Learn**English**
WithAfrica

SHORT STORY

The Departure Lounge

LEVEL B1-B2

Reading Comprehension and Vocabulary Worksheets

By
Thandi Ngwira Gatignol

CONTENTS

FOREWORD

There are many advantages to reading short stories when you are learning English.

First of all, short stories are 'short', therefore you a get a sense of accomplishment much quicker than when you read a novel.

Secondly, you encounter different interesting characters and you can put yourself in their shoes. This can be done by appropriating the way they think or talk. Vocabulary is thus easier to grasp and digest.

Thirdly, language and grammatical structures are seen in context. Hence, you will gain a deeper understanding of how words, tenses and punctuation work together to form meaning.

Finally, reading short stories gives you access to valuable cultural information about a people, country or continent.

I hope that **The Departure Lounge** meets your expectations and fosters your own creativity.

Thandi Ngwira Gatignol, Founder (Learn English With Africa)

The Departure Lounge

I am at the airport. The plane will leave in an hour. I knit to pass time. A man with an ashy face enters the room. He is flail and sickly-looking. The baton on his hip encumbers him, you can tell from the way he walks. His uniform is neatly ironed and the straight lines on his trousers jut out like fish bones. My eyes are drawn to his feet, the sturdiest part of his body that allows him to stand and address the passengers in a dignified way.

"Excuse me Ladies and Gentlemen," he announces, "May you please go outside to identify your luggage."

The silence is stifling. He wants us to stand up. No one does. I do not fail to notice the questioning glances, the unamused mutterings, the groans. We expect clarification, some form of explanation as to why we should execute this order. The man does not open his mouth again. He instead shuffles to the other end of the room. The door leading to the runway is opened by his bony hands. When the humid air hits his face, he flinches and even his boots seem to fail him.

I pull out another ball of yarn, my eyes carefully avoiding the rest of the passengers. I hear the rustling of plastic bags. I continue knitting. The noise is coming from my neighbour, an elderly man with sleek hair. He is putting away his newspaper. He then stands up, stretches his back and yawns loudly. I look up again. I catch his wife staring at him. She is draped in a green beaded satin sari and she looks much younger than him. He smiles at her and I realise that he cannot help it. Even in her anger, her beauty is dazzling. He pats her shoulders lightly, his eyes imploring forgiveness, and with his well-manicured hands beckons her to follow him. She softens under his cheerful disposition. They leave together after a few minutes, heading towards the exit where they are to identify their luggage.

Slowly, we all rouse to action. I carefully put my knitting needles on the patched leather seat behind me. I make sure the yarn is disentangled. It takes longer than I thought. I keep on my task. When I finally finish, there are only three women left in the room. They are quarrelling in hushed voices and I do not wish to be entangled in their affairs. I quickly grab my handbag and walk out.

I am equally surprised by the heat that slaps my face when I step onto the tarmac. The hot air sucks my breath. I lose my bearings; I panic. I want to regain my composure but I can't. I blink my eyes tightly to block the sharp rays of sunlight. My efforts are futile; the furnace is unbearable. I bring my heavily ringed fingers to my face to remove the rivulets of sweat that are already flooding my cracked skin.

The cold from the metal is of momentary comfort but my body soon recognises the treachery. I am drenched in no time and my dress sticks to me as if I have just come out of a heavy downpour. The position is unpleasant and I worry about the smell, and the discomfort I will have to endure on the plane when the air conditioner will freeze me to the bone.

I am brought back to my senses when the man in uniform speaks to us again. We are clustered on the tarmac, facing him. He is standing in front of a row of suitcases and travelling bags that are propped up against the lime-painted flaking walls.

"We will soon start the identification process. Come nearer and point at your property."

He has no need to raise his voice. We all understand the gravity of the situation. In silence, we form a queue. As before, the elderly couple is the first to act. They solemnly move forward. They go past a few pieces of luggage and stop in front of a large grey hard-shell four-wheel suitcase. It is battered and this is obviously its last trip abroad. The woman's expensive sari jars against this cheap-looking belonging. I fight against a feeling of disappointment. The couple is unaffected though. The husband even grasps the suitcase handle for a short while, proudly claiming ownership of this disgrace.

We follow suit, the other forty passengers or so, asserting our pride, shame or disaffection, depending on what we have or have not. Fortunately, the ordeal is over in a few minutes and we file back into the stale departure lounge. I am glad to escape the heat outside but coming back here feels abnormal. I wish we had gone straight to the plane. The order of events is illogical and unnatural.

The progress is slow. Everyone seems to take their time. The straggling of clammy feet is annoying, the stagnant air suffocating. A woman in a bright overflowing *bubu* presses against me, involuntarily pushing me forward. I stiffen to brace myself against the onslaught.

"There's no room in front."

She does not respond.

"Your reed bag is digging into my back," I say, a bit louder this time. When nothing happens, I turn to give her a death stare. She shakes her head sideways, a gesture ripe with disapproval, and keeps on moving. I see she does not understand. I decide to give her some space. She outsmarts me by thrusting me to the side with her elbow.

"What's the rush?" I yell between my teeth.

"A grown-up girl like you walking like a snail!" she sneers. "Be energetic *chemwali.*"

"Don't mind her," a man whispers in my right ear. "She can get violent."

Her face seems familiar though. It takes me a few seconds to remember where I first saw her. She is one of the women who had been arguing in the departure lounge. I conclude that she is ill-mannered. In fact, it is not hard to follow the man's advice. I stop and let a few people pass by before I proceed to regain my seat.

By then, I am in a bad mood. I resist the urge to complain when I see the throng of flies that has now colonised the place. They hover about, grating on my nerves. I am helpless against them, and they know it those flies. This is why they keep on coming back, increasing their numbers until the only noise we hear is the drone of their hunger.

A young black girl in her late teens pulls out something blue from her multi-coloured ethnic bag.

"You want some?" she asks.

For a moment, I think that her offer isn't directed at me but her unflinching gaze decides me. I hold out my hand gratefully to receive the Wrigley's Winterfresh gum. I know this will bring little relief to my parched throat but I remove the silver wrapping quickly and slide the strong mint into my mouth.

"Thank you," I say to the girl. She smiles at me generously. I wonder if she is Malawian from her faded torn jeans. It isn't just her attire that differentiates her from the rest of us. It is her self-confidence that mostly reveals her strong Western background. The tone of her voice is clear and loud. Her pure American accent is unmistakable. Her easy manners do speak volumes. She laughs loudly with anyone and at anything. The innate fear of elders that I have so often observed in my peers is nonexistent in her character. And her hair is natural and very short like a boy's. We strictly have nothing in common.

I go back to my knitting. No one has tampered with it apart from the flies that continuously frustrate my efforts. I unfold the unfinished light blue scarf and start straightening it. The pattern is simple but stylish. It's a pity my winter coat is brown. I will certainly end up looking like a Christmas tree.

My back is now slightly bent and my fingers are working furiously, twirling the thick yarn around the needles at a speed which even surprises me. The scarf grows in length and beauty. I am so absorbed in this activity that I do not notice the escalating voices. I ignore these distractions and continue with my task. A shriek coming from the opposite side of the room jolts me back to reality. I raise my head and I am irritated to see the flail man again. He is saying something to the outspoken *bubu*-clad woman. It is his boots that remind me of his face. I drop my gaze and try to concentrate on the knitting.

"Keep quiet! Don't you see that you are in a distinguished place?" He is now wielding the baton in his hands and the threatening gesture quietens everyone in the room. I look at my watch. We should be boarding the plane in a moment.

"What's your name?" he asks.

"NyaNkhonjera," she answers. Both tone and demeanor are subdued at present.

"Where are you going?"

"To London," she says.

The officer nods and asks for her passport. She hands him the black document, her fingers slightly shaking.

"What are you going to do there?" he asks, leafing through the new passport without reading its contents. I put my knitting in my handbag. Slowly.

"I'm..."

"Wait a minute. Where did you say you were going?"

"To London. Didn't I just say so?"

I lift my head. NyaNkhonjera is taking off her light sweater. She uses it to wipe her glistening brow. Her movements are defiant unlike a few minutes before.

"What are you going to do there?"

"I'm going to visit my sister."

A cadaverous smile crosses the officer's emaciated face. He reminds me of his first entrance in the room. I take a quick glance at my watch again.

"*Oh, ho*, I see." He nods his head, smiling still. "Where do you come from?"

"Can I be of any help? I'm also a Londoner." A middle-aged white woman, with a Java Print *chitenje* carelessly wrapped around her slim waist, blurts out. I wonder how Justine and Leila would react if I arrived at Charles de Gaulle Airport in the same gear.

"Don't worry madam," he says in an ingratiating tone. "Everything is under control madam."

The lady is not convinced though. She stands up and goes to sit next to NyaNkhonjera.

"If you need any help, I'm here."

Her gestures are soft, earnest and welcoming. I imagine what she has just been doing in our country. Taking care of orphans, visiting sick people, teaching aimless street children, finding new sources of energy that will stop us from senselessly cutting down our own trees. My heart shrinks with shame. I imagine her next trip. She will bring more people, more money, more energy to help us rise above our poverty and pettiness. I imagine how she will impersonate this fight, just as she is doing right now with NyaNkhonjera. My eyes linger on this improbable friendship until watching the two women becomes a burden.

The officer's gaze weighs down on them too. He coughs energetically, straining the muscles on his throat. Even swallowing the phlegm requires incredible effort on his part.

"Be careful next time," he growls as he shuffles his way out of the room. The two offenders do not pay attention to him. I realise that he is leaving with her passport.

"Give her back her passport," I shout and immediately try to cover my mistake by putting a hand on my mouth.

"You forgot to give her back her travelling documents," I mumble afterwards, wishing I had remained quiet. Hot blood rushes through my veins. I feel like I have just been running a never-ending marathon. I try to quieten the thumping in my heart by concentrating on the thump of his shiny boots as they draw nearer to where I am sitting. I am gasping for breath.

"Here you are," the gnarled fingers reach out to me. "Tell her to be more careful next time."

After he is gone, I cannot fail to notice NyaNkhonjera's smile as she stands up to fetch her passport. I am filled with indescribable warmth as I meet her halfway to give her back what is so important to her. I regain my seat, forgetting the fear that had previously assailed me. I heave a sigh of true relief and hopeful expectations. For the first time in my life, I know what it feels like to behave like a real human being.

THE END

VOCABULARY

1. **DEFINITIONS (PART ONE): Find the meanings of the following Adjectives in a unilingual Dictionary.**

a. Flail: ....

....

b. Ashy: ....

....

c. Cheerful: ....

....

d. Dazzling:. ....

....

e. Well-manicured: ....

....

f. Ill-mannered:. ....

....

g. Outspoken:. ....

....

h. Emaciated:. ....

....

i. Aimless: ....

....

j. Cadaverous: ....

....

2. **DEFINITIONS (PART TWO): Find the meanings of the following Adjectives in a unilingual Dictionary.**

a. Beaded: . . . .

. . . .

b. Patched: . . . .

. . . .

c. Battered:. . . . .

. . . .

d. Multi-coloured: . . . .

. . . .

e. Cheap-looking: . . . .

. . . .

f. Overflowing: . . . .

. . . .

g. Faded:. . . . .

. . . .

h. Torn:. . . . .

. . . .

i. Stylish: . . . .

. . . .

j. Light: . . . .

. . . .

k. Shiny: . . . .

. . . .

3. **SYNONYMS:** Find the words that have the same meaning as the Adjectives below.

Word	Synonym	Word	Synonym
Bony		Irritated	
Dignified		Distinguished	
Large		Earnest	
Stagnant		Ingratiating	
Helpless		Careful	
Young		Important	

4. **ANTONYMS:** Find the words that have the opposite meaning of the Adjectives below.

Word	Antonym	Word	Antonym
Stifling		Abnormal	
Entangled		Slow	
Surprised		Strong	
Unbearable		Clammy	
Unpleasant		Annoying	
Heavy		Slim	

5. **WORD SEARCH:** Find the words that are related to airports.

Y	U	Y	P	K	P	B	S	D	H	E	E	S	T	S
A	A	I	A	C	L	A	E	R	Y	G	G	M	L	H
W	R	S	S	A	A	G	C	A	A	A	A	E	E	O
N	R	S	S	S	N	G	U	O	I	G	G	T	B	P
U	I	A	E	H	E	A	R	B	R	G	G	I	R	A
R	V	P	N	M	V	G	I	E	H	U	U	D	O	T
B	A	G	G	A	G	E	T	R	O	L	L	E	Y	T
D	L	N	E	C	S	W	Y	U	S	N	D	T	E	E
U	S	I	R	H	T	R	O	T	T	O	E	I	V	N
T	B	D	S	I	E	A	F	R	E	Y	K	B	N	D
Y	O	R	G	N	W	P	F	A	S	R	C	I	O	A
F	A	A	G	E	A	P	I	P	S	R	E	H	C	N
R	R	O	D	P	R	E	C	E	B	A	H	O	P	T
E	D	B	Z	U	D	R	E	D	S	C	C	R	F	L
E	G	N	U	O	L	E	R	U	T	R	A	P	E	D

AIR HOSTESS	DEPARTURE BOARD
ARRIVALS BOARD	DEPARTURE LOUNGE
BAGGAGE	DUTY-FREE
BAGGAGE TROLLEY	PASSENGERS
BAGGAGE WRAPPER	PLANE
BOARDING PASS	PROHIBITED ITEMS
CARRY-ON LUGGAGE	RUNWAY
CASH MACHINE	SECURITY OFFICER
CHECKED LUGGAGE	SHOP ATTENDANT
CONVEYOR BELT	STEWARD

6. SENSES VOCABULARY: What sense comes to your mind when you see the following words? Fill in the table below.

Eyes, silence, stifling, glances, groans, shuffle, humid, rustling, noise, draped, dazzling, pat, hushed, grab, heat, blink, finger, skin, cold, smell, freeze, identification, mint, loudly, voice, shriek, notice, see, gaze, quiet, look, read, cheap-looking, grasp, suffocating, stale, press, push, whisper, gum, hear

Sound	Sight	Smell	Touch	Taste

7. **WRITING: Write sentences using the following expressions.**

a. To rouse to action:. . . . .

. . . .

b. To keep on task:. . . . .

. . . .

c. To regain one's composure: . . . .

. . . .

d. To lose one's bearings: . . . .

. . . .

e. To jar against: . . . .

. . . .

f. To be clustered around something: . . . .

. . . .

g. To brace oneself against:. . . . .

. . . .

h. To resist the urge to: . . . .

. . . .

i. To be absorbed in something: . . . .

. . . .

j. To drop one's gaze: . . . .

. . . .

k. To leaf through something: . . . .

. . . .

GENERAL COMPREHENSION

1. **GENERAL COMPREHENSION: Read the short story once again and answer the questions below.**

a. What is the title of the short story?: . . . .
. . . .
. . . .

b. What is the story about?: . . . .
. . . .
. . . .

c. Imagine another title for the short story: . . . .
. . . .
. . . .

d. Who is the narrator?:. . . . .

e. How old can she be?:. . . . .

f. How can you describe the narrator in a few words?:. . .
. . . .
. . . .

g. Where does the story take place?: . . . .

h. What are the other places that are mentioned in the story?: . . . .
. . . .
. . . .

i. Pick out two other major characters in the short story and describe them: . . . .
. . . .
. . . .

DETAILED COMPREHENSION

1. **DETAILED COMPREHENSION: Read the short story once again, paying closer attention to how it was written, and answer the questions below.**
   TRUE OR FALSE: Say if the following sentences are TRUE or FALSE. Justify your answer.

a. The airport in this short story is welcoming:. . . . .
   . . . .
   . . . .

b. The security officer looks very healthy: . . . .
   . . . .
   . . . .

c. The security officer asks the passengers to board the plane right away:
   . . . .
   . . . .

d. The narrator feels uncomfortable:
   . . . .
   . . . .

e. A woman from New York comes to NyaNkhonjera's rescue:
   . . . .
   . . . .

f. The security officer goes away with NyaNkhonjera's passport:
   . . . .

WRITE FULL ANSWERS TO THE FOLLOWING QUESTIONS:

a. How can you characterize the narrator's behaviour at the beginning of the story?: . . . .

. . . .

. . . .

. . . .

. . . .

b. How does her behaviour change as the story advances?:

. . . .

. . . .

. . . .

. . . .

c. What can you say about the security officer's behaviour?:. . . . .

. . . .

. . . .

. . . .

. . . .

d. How does the narrator cope with the challenges in her environment? . . . .

. . . .

. . . .

. . . .

. . . .

e. In your opinion, why is the atmosphere in this airport so emotionally-charged? . . . .

. . . .

. . . .

. . . .

f.   What could make the situation better?: . . . .

. . . .

. . . .

. . . .

. . . .

g.   What do you make of NyaNkhonjera's behaviour? Do
you think that she deserves the help that was given to
her at the end of the story?: . . . .

. . . .

. . . .

. . . .

. . . .

. . . .

h.   How does the narrator describe the girl who shares
her chewing gum with her? Is her description accu-
rate?: . . . .

. . . .

. . . .

. . . .

. . . .

i.   Describe the old couple at the beginning of the story:

. . . .

. . . .

. . . .

. . . .

j.   How is this airport's departure lounge different from
or similar to the ones you usually encounter?: . . . .

. . . .

. . . .

. . . .

. . . .

WRITTEN EXPRESSION

1.

<u>PAY ATTENTION TO THE FOLLOWING POINTS:</u>

a. **Plot or Structure:** Think about how your story unfolds and develops in time. What will be the.....?:
   Exposition:. . . . .
   Rising action:. . . . .
   Climax:. . . . .
   Falling action: . . . .
   Resolution:. . . . .

b. **Vocabulary:** Avoid repeating words unless it is a deliberate, stylistic device. Use descriptive language and show instead of telling.

c. **Grammar:** Pay attention to how you write. Think about tenses, syntax, spelling and punctuation.

d. **Originality:** Make your story as interesting as possible. It should be worth the read.

WRITTEN EXPRESSION CHECKLIST	
My story has a title.	✓
My story has a plot.	✓
I have varied the vocabulary.	✓
I have paid attention to grammar (tenses, syntax, spelling and punctuation.)	✓
My story is original and interesting.	✓

NOTES

IN LOVING MEMORY OF

James Chamahiya Ngwira
(31ˢᵗ October, 1955-23ʳᵈ February, 1995)
Maggie Ngwira *nee* Mhango
(19ᵗʰ July, 1959-23ʳᵈ February, 1995)
Nicholas Chamahiya Ngwira
(30ᵗʰ October, 1962-23ʳᵈ February, 1995)
Frida Ngwira *nee* Itimu
(12ᵗʰ June, 1960-23ʳᵈ February, 1995)
Manasseh Chamahiya Ngwira
(22ⁿᵈ July, 1985-04ᵗʰ October, 2018)

May your departed souls continue resting in peace.

www.ingramcontent.com/pod-product-compliance
Lightning Source LLC
LaVergne TN
LVHW041445170726
843492LV00008B/2824